INSIDE A
TELEPHONE

JOHN BASSETT

GROLIER
EDUCATIONAL

ABOUT THIS SET

Have you ever wanted to look inside a machine to see how it works? The "Inside a..." books help you do just that. With the help of photographs and illustrations, the workings of many machines, some everyday, some not so common, are revealed.

Each book gives you the history behind its subject: for example, what rockets were used for before they took people into space, or when the first web sites were created. That is followed by a large illustration that takes you inside the fascinating things covered in the series. The engines, the moving parts, and the control systems are all on display.

The main section of the "Inside a..." books explains how all the different parts work together and what they are used for. Fact files throughout each book highlight special features and interesting information. For even better understanding, some of the scientific points raised are illustrated by activities, such as model-making and experiments.

The final part of each book gives you a glimpse into the future. What will the jet planes, stoves, and televisions of the future look like? Find out inside.

New words that you might not understand are explained in the glossary; and if you are looking for something in particular, you can find it in the index. Most importantly, just have fun!

Published 2001 by
Grolier Educational, Sherman Turnpike, Danbury, Connecticut 06816

© 2001 Brown Partworks Ltd

Library of Congress Cataloging-in-Publication Data

Inside a--
    p.cm.
  Includes index.
  Contents: v. 1. Helicopter — v. 2. Car — v. 3. Construction machine — v. 4. Television — v. 5. Powerboat — v. 6. Skyscraper — v. 7 Rocket — v. 8. High-speed train — v. 9. Clock — v. 10. Compact disk — v. 11. Jet plane — v. 12. Web site — v. 13. Satellite — v. 14. Telephone — v. 15. Stove — v. 16. Computer.
  ISBN 0-7172-9521-4 (set : alk. paper)
  1. Machinery—Juvenile literature. 2. Technology—Juvenile literature. [1. Machinery. 2. Technology.] I. Grolier Educational Corporation.

TJ147 .I57 2000
600—dc21
                                        00-029415
                                            CIP

FOR BROWN PARTWORKS
Project editor: Roland Hall
Consultant: Dr. Derek Smith
Designer: Sarah Williams
Illustrators: Matthew White (main artwork), Mark Walker
Managing editor: Anne O'Daly
Picture researcher: Becky Cox

Printed in Italy.

Contents

History of telecommunications and message sending

Sending messages quickly over long distances became more important in the 18th and 19th centuries as people traveled further around the world. At that time long-distance messages could only be sent as far as people could see or hear.

In 1837 two British men, Charles Wheatstone (1802–1875) and Sir William Cooke (1806–1879), realized that moving a conductor (a device that conducts electricity) in and out of a magnetic field could create a coded signal. When a conductor is moved close to a magnet, it produces an electrical current that can be sent along an electrical wire. With this knowledge they developed what became known as the "telegraph" system. It was originally used to send signals on the railways.

Alexander Graham Bell with a more advanced telephone than the one pictured left.

In that same year American Samuel Morse (1791–1872) developed a method of communication using a code. It used a series of short and long signals (dots and dashes) of electricity to represent the letters of the alphabet. Morse code was used to send the new telegraph messages. At that time messages could only be sent within one

The first "telephone." Bell used it to send the first ever speech messages via electricity.

THIS MODEL OF BELL'S FIRST TELEPHONE IS A DUPLICATE OF THE INSTRU-MENT THROUGH WHICH SPEECH SOUNDS WERE FIRST TRANSMITTED ELECTRICALLY. 1875.

country, but in 1866 American Cyrus Field (1819–1892) laid the first transatlantic telegraph cable, enabling messages to be sent across continents. The telegraph needed an operator at both ends to code the messages—people could not talk to each other directly.

Alexander Graham Bell (1847–1922), a Scotsman living in America, was a specialist in the education of deaf children. While he was working on a system to improve the telegraph, he discovered a way to send voices over wires by electricity. In 1876 he made the world's first telephone call to his assistant by saying, "Mr. Watson, come here, I want you."

In 1878 the first telephone exchange opened in New Haven, Connecticut. It had 21 subscribers (people with telephones), and one of them was the famous writer Mark Twain (1835–1910).

Wireless signals

In 1895 the Italian inventor Guglielmo Marconi (1874–1937) sent messages by changing electrical signals into radio waves, enabling messages to be sent without wires.

Modern optical fibers use light to send a large number of signals as a digital code with no interference. The first telephone messages were sent through optical fibers in 1977. The International Services Digital Network (ISDN) was launched in 1988 and is used to send digital-only signals along optical fibers. The first fiber-optic cable to cross the Atlantic Ocean was laid in 1989. It is capable of carrying more than 40,000 telephone conversations at the same time. In the 21st century more telephone conversations are being sent via communications satellites.

The telex—or teleprinter exchange—was developed in 1932 and was the first way of sending automatically printed messages. Automatic typewriters were used to print and send messages using electrical codes.

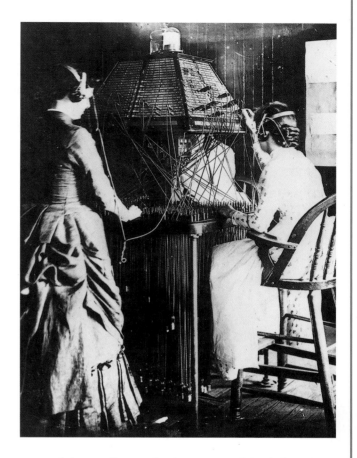

One of the earliest telephone switchboards—the "lampshade switchboard," first used in 1882.

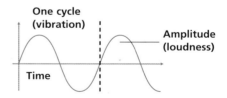

Sound travels through the air in waves. Changes of frequency (number of cycles per second) make different sounds. The changes in sound waves cause differing electrical currents to be sent along telephone lines.

Fast vibrations make high-pitched sounds (left), and slow vibrations make low-pitched sounds (right).

Inside a telephone

When the handset is lifted, it allows electricity to flow into the telephone. A hook switch is released, and it initially connects the person using the telephone to the telephone network. In a cordless telephone the signal first passes from the handset to the base as a radio signal before communicating with the telephone exchange.

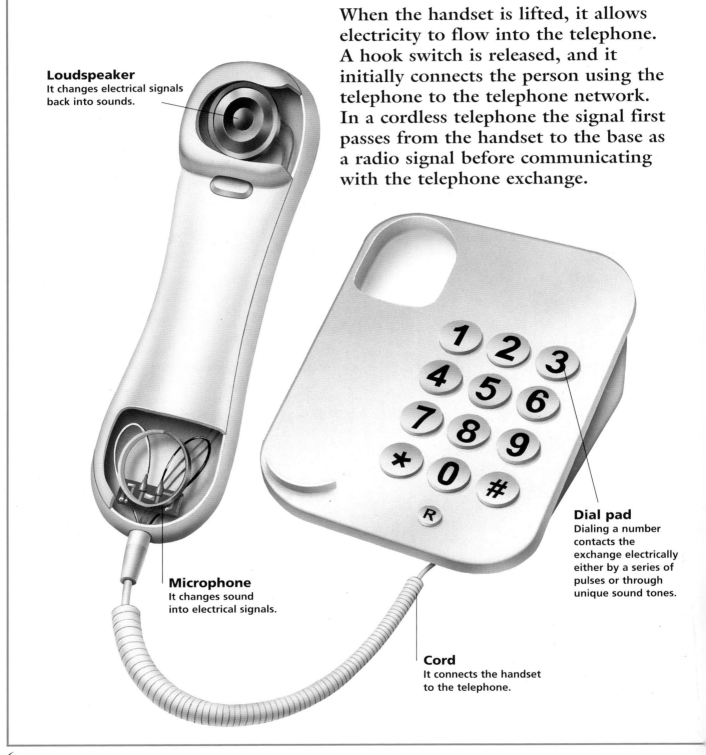

Loudspeaker
It changes electrical signals back into sounds.

Microphone
It changes sound into electrical signals.

Dial pad
Dialing a number contacts the exchange electrically either by a series of pulses or through unique sound tones.

Cord
It connects the handset to the telephone.

Loudspeaker

PCB
A printed circuit board holds all of the electronic circuits in the telephone.

MEM
555 1234

Display
It tells you which number you dialed and other information.

Receiver
It communicates between the telephone and the base unit.

ST
ME
RCL
PWR
1
2
4
5
7
8
*
0

FACT FILE

⟲ Most modern telephones have memories. You program the telephone with your favorite numbers, and you only need to press a few keys to dial them.

⟲ Old telephones had handles on the side to generate electricity to make your telephone line ring at the local exchange.

⟲ Some telephones display the number of the person who is calling you when the phone is ringing. If you have that number in your telephone's memory, the phone will display the name.

Base unit
It contains a charger for the battery inside the handset and connects the telephone to the exchange.

Silicon chip
It controls the telephone.

Microphone
It changes the sound waves and passes them to the receiver.

How calls are sent and received

The first stage of making a telephone call is lifting the receiver. It releases the hook switch on a telephone; turning the handset on has the same effect on a cordless telephone. It lets electric current flow through the telephone, and it connects the person making the call to the network.

Older telephones have a wheel that is used to dial the numbers. It turns on a plate with the numbers from 1 to 9, with 0 as a final number. The caller dials by putting their finger in a hole in the wheel and turning the dial until it reaches a stop point. The wheel then returns to its original position. As it returns, a series of electrical pulses are sent along the line. The distance between the finger hole and the stop decides how many pulses are sent. Push-button or touch-tone telephones have a pad with numbers from 1 to 9 plus 0. When a button is pushed on the number pad, a unique pair of electronic tones is produced. This is known as dual-tone multifrequency signaling.

Whichever telephone is used, the signals arrive at the exchange, and the receiving

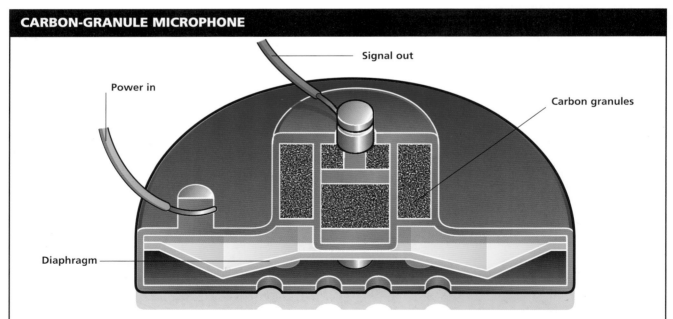

CARBON-GRANULE MICROPHONE

Signal out

Power in

Carbon granules

Diaphragm

The carbon-granule microphone converts sounds into electrical signals that are then sent along wires. The diaphragm moves when hit by sound waves, and this compresses the carbon granules, producing a varying electrical signal.

Dialing a number on an old-style telephone. Modern telephones send sounds (tones).

diaphragm is a gold-plated brass dome. It sits in a chamber containing small grains of carbon. When the diaphragm vibrates, the dome moves and presses the carbon grains. The more the dome squeezes the grains, the more current flows. If the pressure reduces, the grains separate, and less current flows. This current flow carries the electrical pattern of the sound to the speaker or receiver.

A telephone speaker is made up of three parts. A very light cylinder with a thin wire coil wound around it becomes an electromagnet when electrical current flows through it. This electromagnet is placed next to a permanent magnet. They are separated by a small gap filled with air. As the electrical signal travels into the coil, the magnets attract or repel each other. This moves the coil, which makes a thin paper cone or diaphragm vibrate and causes sound waves that are directed toward the ear.

telephone number is called. Electricity flows to the bell in the telephone, which makes the ringer activate. This tells you that someone is trying to call you.

Speaking and listening

Sounds must be converted to electrical impulses in order to be sent through wires. A microphone is used for the sound input and a speaker for the sound output. A telephone handset has a microphone or transmitter and a speaker or receiver. The most common type of microphone in a telephone is a carbon-granule microphone. Sound enters a carbon-granule microphone and meets a thin piece of aluminum called the diaphragm. It is tight like a drum skin and vibrates when sound hits it. Under the

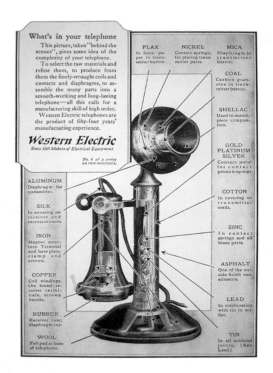

This advertisement is from 1923. Although it was a simple telephone, it had many components.

Telephone networks

When your telephone wires leave the house, the telephone becomes part of the telephone network. It is a system of wires, fiber-optic cables, and microwave transmitters that carry the signals.

The first part of the network is called the local loop. The electrical signal from the telephone travels through a twisted pair of copper wires. The wires are twisted to cut down on interference. Outside the house the pairs of twisted wires are wound together to make a cable, which is buried underground or fastened to telephone poles. This cable is connected to a central office, where each pair

Telephone poles are the most common means of connecting your telephone to the local loop.

of wires is joined to the local switching machine. Each switch contains wiring for up to 80,000 telephones. If a call is made between two telephones connected to the same switch, then the call is within the local loop. A call made outside the local loop needs to be sent by a cable called a trunk. It transfers signals from one local loop to another local loop.

In modern telephone systems 96 twisted-pair lines from one neighborhood are fed to the central office using a subscriber loop carrier (SLC). It is a small box or underground vault where 24 telephone circuits are combined together onto one special twisted pair of lines called a T or T1 carrier. The SLC translates the electrical signals from the twisted wires into digital signals. The digital signals are then combined or "multiplexed." Multiplexing is when many signals are sent at almost the same time along

This New York street, pictured in 1880, is already lined with telephone poles.

the same wire, making it easier and cheaper to send a greater number of signals.

Carrying the calls

Analog telephone systems combine signals using frequency-division multiplexing. Different frequency signals carrying different calls are transmitted together.

Modern digital systems use a system called time-division multiplexing in which the telephone signal is digital: it is sent as a stream of binary numbers or bits. The messages are broken down into sections, and they are sent at different time intervals, weaving the information as they are sent. Each telephone signal requires the sending of 64,000 bits per second. When the multiplexed signals reach the central office, they are then sorted into separate signals—demultiplexed—and are then transmitted on to their separate numbers.

A SIMPLE TELEPHONE

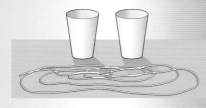

1 You will need a length of string (about 20 feet [6m]) and two clean, empty plastic pots.

2 Make a hole in the bottom of each pot just small enough to push one end of the string through. Push one end of the string through each pot, and tie a knot in it.

3 Give one pot to a friend, and stand far enough away from each other that the string stays tight. Talk to your friend through your pot while they listen through their pot.

You can hear what the other person is saying because your voices make the tight string vibrate. Sound waves are vibrations in air. A real telephone uses electricity to send its sound waves.

Digital and analog

In the 1970s the old analog system of sending electrical signals started to be replaced by the newer technology of the faster and more reliable digital system.

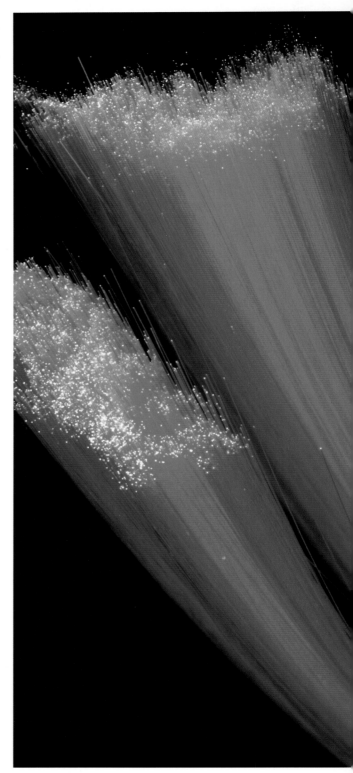

Electrical signals sent along wires lose quality through interference (something else gets in the way). Digital systems reduce the amount of interference by converting the signal into a binary code. This conversion is carried out by an anlog-to-digital convertor (ADC). The convertor measures the heights of the waves of electrical current about 8,000 times every second. These measurements become a binary code of 1s and 0s. The electrical current is now a code represented as a series of pulses. "1" means that current flows, while "0" means the current stops. This is known as pulse-code modulation (PCM). Because each pulse is very short, the pulses of a number of telephone messages can be interwoven (mixed together) as they are sent.

The best way to send digitally coded messages is through fiber-optic cables. They are very fine strands of glass that carry messages very quickly as flashes of light. Fiber-optic cables can carry any signal that has been digitally encoded. As well as voices, this includes computer information, pictures, and written text. More information can be sent at the same time. Signals traveling over long distances in copper cables have to be boosted to improve the quality. Digital signals do not fade as quickly and do not require as many boosters.

Fiber-optic cables, like this one, are the best type of cable for sending digitally coded messages.

This computer and telephone setup is a complete digital communication system.

It is important to reduce the risk of messages becoming confused. Digital communication networks use a set of instructions that are known as digital communications protocols. Different signals are sent through the network to check that messages are going to the correct destination. This is known as electronic routing. The sequence of information being sent is also checked to make sure there are no signal mistakes. This is known as error checking.

Many old copper cables are being dug up and replaced with fiber-optic ones, like this.

Converting signals

When the encoded signal reaches the receiving end, the light pulses are picked up by a photodetector. It turns the light signals back into electrical signals. They are fed to a decoder, which changes the binary code back into an electrical signal that either matches the vibrations from the caller's mouthpiece or re-creates the computer file, pictures, or text.

FACT FILE

⭕ **Not all frequency sounds can be sent over telephone wires. To hear some sounds that cannot be sent, look at this web site:**

http://www.howstuffworks.com/telephone3.htm

Communicating with the world

Signals are carried over long distances by electrical or fiber-optic cables, or they are sent by microwave transmitters and communications satellites.

Coaxial cables carry trunk telephone calls. These cables have a central copper wire surrounded by an outer copper conductor sleeve. Trunk cables carry hundreds of thousands of calls at high frequencies.

If a signal has to travel a long way, it becomes weaker. To avoid losing the signal, amplifiers boost it every 1½ miles (2km). Cables either run underground or from telephone poles. Underground cables are covered with a sleeve that is filled with compressed air. This keeps water from seeping in and destroying the signal.

This mixture of aerials and dishes make up a communication station in England.

Under the sea
Undersea cables carry signals across the ocean from one continent to another. The cables are laid by remote-control submarines, known as sea plows. Early underwater cables broke regularly, but modern cables are protected by polyethylene insulation. They follow routes that avoid hazards such as strong currents and fishing areas where trawlers could catch the cable in their nets. The cables are monitored

This is an undersea telegraph cable. The diver is inspecting it before it is covered over.

(50km) apart. Microwaves travel in straight lines, and receiving towers cannot be located behind buildings, or the signal will be lost. Microwaves can carry both analog or digital signals, but they can be affected by interference from snow, rain, and other bad weather conditions.

Communications satellites orbit the Earth at heights of about 22,500 miles (36,000km) above the Equator. They travel at a speed so that each orbit takes exactly 24 hours. This makes them appear to remain in the same place above the Earth. It is known as geo-stationary orbit. Each satellite collects signals from a given area, known as its footprint. Microwave signals from the Earth are sent to the satellite from large transmission dish aerials. The signals are amplified by the satellites and then fed back down to other receiving dishes.

Old cables are being replaced by fiber-optic ones, and in 1997 the Fiber-optic Link Around the Globe (FLAG) was completed. It covers a distance of 16,800 miles (27,000km).

by ships on the surface to make sure that there are no breaks. If a break is found, a remote-controlled submarine is sent to the seabed. It uncovers the cable by blowing a high pressure jet of air. It then pulls the cable back to the surface so that it can be repaired.

Sometimes long-distance telephone signals on land are sent by microwave radio transmission. Microwaves are high-frequency radio waves. The signal is converted into a microwave and sent from one transmission tower to another until it arrives at its destination. The towers are normally 30 miles

This shows the laying of the first telegraph cable between England and France. It was in 1851.

Exchanges, numbers, and switching

Old telephone switchboards had an operator. When a telephone receiver was lifted, a bulb would light up to show the operator who wanted to make the call. They would ask the caller for the number and plug a connection into a socket for the number requested.

Engineers are checking that the switches at this telephone exchange are working properly.

As the number of telephones increased, new systems were developed. The first automatic way of switching calls was with the electromechanical switchgear developed by Almon Strowger in 1888, and it was popular for many years. It contained a bank of fixed electrical contacts in a semicircle around a moving selector arm. The number was called step by step. When the first digit was dialed, it sent the arm up to a bank of contacts matching the digit. The arm then turned to find a free contact. This connected it to the next bank of circuits. If the arm could not find a free circuit, the caller heard the busy tone. This process continued until the final selector made contact with the line of the number being called. If the selector accidentally stuck on an incorrect contact, then you got a crossed line.

Modern dialing uses electronic telephone exchanges. In them the audible tones from dialing are received by electronic circuit boards. Microchips on these boards understand the tones and make the correct connections automatically. Electronic circuits have no moving parts, so they are more reliable than the electromechanical switchgear.

FACT FILE

⭕ Some telephone numbers are free to call all the time. The emergency services numbers for the police, ambulance, and fire brigade are the most common, but coast guards and mountain rescue are important as well.

⭕ Look out for office switchboards and other manual systems of telephone switching.

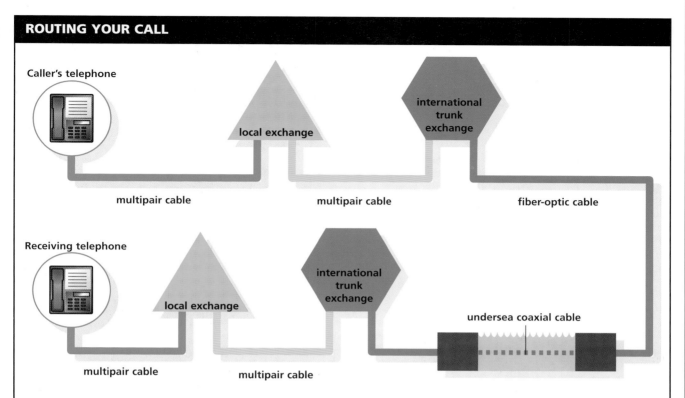

ROUTING YOUR CALL

Caller's telephone

local exchange

international trunk exchange

multipair cable

multipair cable

fiber-optic cable

Receiving telephone

local exchange

international trunk exchange

undersea coaxial cable

multipair cable

multipair cable

When you make an international phone call, the electrical signals are sent from your home to your local exchange and then to the international exchange. Then they travel across the ocean and through another set of exchanges until you reach the telephone that you dialed.

Name or number?

Every telephone now has a number, but originally telephones were identified only by the name of the user. To connect to another person with a telephone, you would speak to the operator, who would put you through to the person you wanted to talk to. Sometimes your operator would have to connect to other operators as well. As more people got phones, the directories that listed the users grew.

Using only names became confusing, so each entry was given a number. Part of the telephone number is an area code. These codes were originally letters showing where the telephone exchange was, like PEnnsylvania. These exchange names were changed to numbers in the 1960s. This meant that letters were no longer needed.

This is an old electromechanical switchgear. Modern switching systems are solely electronic.

Construction, materials, and the shape of the telephone

Since its invention the telephone has changed shape. Alexander Graham Bell's telephone was made up of a single wooden box with a hole in one end, which was used for both listening and speaking.

With those old telephones it was difficult to hold a conversation. The caller had to lift the heavy box to their ear and then move it back to their mouth to speak. The Butterstamp telephone was designed in 1878.

Right: A modern cordless telephone. The handset is not attached to the base unit.

On it the receiver was attached to the unit by a wire, but it was still used for both listening and speaking.

Some callers had two telephone units linked and used one for speaking and the other for listening. This system of a separate receiver and microphone became the basis for the modern

This was one of the first push-button telephones. It was built in 1974.

telephone. Candlestick telephones had the receiver hanging on a hook on the side. They were heavy and made from brass. The first telephone with a receiver and microphone combined in the handset was known as the skeleton telephone. The legs of the telephone base were electromagnets for a hand generator to power the phone's bell, and the wiring was exposed at the back of the phone.

Interference

Making a call from a noisy public place has always been a problem because a telephone's microphone picks up noise from all around, not just the caller's voice. One early solution—from Thomas Edison's company—was a unit with two listening tubes that the caller put to their ears. Another was the horse collar. The caller placed their face onto a large padded ring to keep their mouth the right distance from the microphone.

Telephone bells needed electricity to make them ring. It came either from a battery or from a small generator—or magneto—that was turned by hand. Magnetos could produce up to 75 volts of electricity. This meant that the body of the telephone needed to be insulated. Insulation also helped cut down the loss of the electrical signal. In 1927 telephones started to be made from Bakelite, a type of plastic. It was hard, molded plastic, which could be shaped into different designs.

Automatic exchanges meant that people no longer needed operators and could dial their own numbers. Telephones were equipped with dials on the front with finger holes, and in 1974 the first telephones with push-button dials were produced. They made dialing numbers much faster and easier.

Modern telephones are made from molded plastic with printed circuit boards replacing the heavy, bulky wiring of the early phones. Most people who use the telephone as part of their work now use headsets rather than

This very old telephone has a handle on the side to generate its own electricity.

handsets to talk. As microphones and earpieces become smaller, they have become lighter and easier to use.

FACT FILE

○ **Some telephones are designed for use by deaf people. These phones have keyboards and videoscreens. People use them by typing the words that they want to say.**

○ **Look at the different telephone poles that are around. See if you can spot microwave towers on hilltops.**

○ **Compare the different phones that you see in people's houses, and see which one you think is the most comfortable to use.**

Fax machines and modems

The very first attempt at sending pictures, documents, and drawings by electricity was in 1866, when Giovanni Caselli (1815–1891) developed a machine in France. It was called the pantelegraphe.

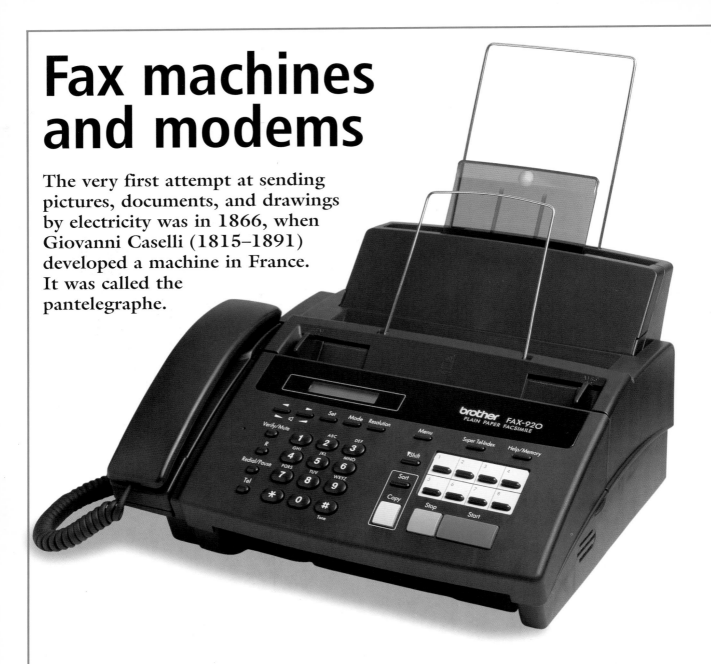

This fax machine has a handset on the side so it can be used as a normal telephone as well.

The pantelegraphe was a huge machine standing 6½ feet (2m) tall. It sent pictures using the telegraph. In one year Caselli transmitted 5,000 documents between the French cities of Paris and Lyon.

It was not until the 1920s that facsimile (fax) transmission machines using telephone wires to send documents came into more regular use. The first machines were used by newspapers to transmit photographs. They were very slow and used a large drum, which turned the document in front of a series of photoelectric cells. A further problem was that these machines could only send pictures to other machines that operated on the same signaling system. It was not until the 1980s that all fax machines worked on the same system.

Inside a fax

The most important parts of a fax machine are the scanner and the modem. First, a document is scanned. The scanner uses a mirror, a lens, and a charge-coupled device (CCD). It is an electronic chip that recognizes the light and dark sections of documents being sent as tiny dots called pixels. These pixels are converted into digital code.

The modem changes digital signals from the fax machine into lower-frequency signals that can be sent on any system. When the signal reaches the receiving fax machine, the modem translates the signal back to its original form.

FIBER-OPTIC CABLE

You will need a length of plastic tube, a box (black inside), and a flashlight.

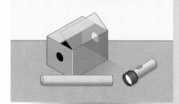

1 Make one hole in the box the same size as the plastic tube, and put one end of the tube in the box. In the other end of the box make a smaller hole.

2 Use the flashlight to send signals to a friend looking in the box. If you have more plastic tube, you could make your cable longer. Try sending signals using Morse code.

This is a fax machine from the 1950s. It took two hours to send a photograph to another machine.

The pantelegraphe was the first machine used to send pictures.

Pay phones

England is famous for its red public telephone boxes, but they are no longer made.

The very first public telephone was in Hartford, Connecticut, in 1889. Coins were dropped into the telephone through a slot at the top.

In 1912 a new payphone with three slots for different values of coin was introduced. When a coin is dropped in the slot, an audible tone is triggered. The size of the coin affects the frequency of the tone. The tone is relayed back to the central telephone office and tells the telephone company how much money has been put into the telephone. If someone tries to use the wrong coin in a payphone, no tone

will be produced, and the coin will be returned. Coinless or "charge-a-call" telephones need a credit card or a charge card to make a call. When the card is put into a slot on the telephone, the magnetic strip on the back of the card is read. This charges calls directly to the card. Other card systems have an account number, which is put in through the telephone dial. A unique password number makes sure that no one else can use the card. Any calls are then charged to the card.

Phone in a box

Public telephones are mounted in telephone booths. The aim of the booth is to protect the user from the weather and cut down the

22

amount of noise from outside. Many modern telephone booths have insulated glass panels to cut out extra noise. The handsets also have adjustable volume controls. Telephone booths are often vandalized, and telephone companies now use armored cords and strengthened polycarbonate handsets in telephones that are regularly damaged.

Some new pay phones have facilities for linking laptop computers or portable fax machines to the telephone. Some of them are equipped with a small video screen and keyboard and can send data as well as voice messages. These phones are also telephone devices for the deaf (TDD), with the screen displaying text messages for deaf people.

Handset
You only need to pick it up if you want to make a voice call

Keyboard
It allows you to write emails or communicate with other services

Payment
You can either insert coins or "swipe" a credit card for payment

Touch screen
It allows you to give the machine instructions by just pressing on the screen

Paper money
You can insert bills in this slot. The machine will recognize how much money you put in

PAYPHONE • INTERNET • EMAIL

Seeing and hearing

For many businesses one problem is traveling long distances to meetings with customers. One way to overcome this is videoconferencing, which allows a group of people to make a telephone call and see each other.

This mobile telephone has a camera in it as well as a tiny screen to see who you are talking to.

Early videoconference systems were very large and needed special rooms, or they had to be moved from room to room, but modern systems are a lot easier to use. Sending pictures through telephone lines takes about the same amount of space (bandwidth) on a telephone cable as 1,400 normal telephone calls. Television pictures are broadcast at a rate of 25 frames (pictures) per second, but most videoconferencing systems cut down the amount of signal by only transmitting every other frame and sending between 10 and 15 frames per second. This means they use less bandwidth.

Image compression can also reduce the amount of image signal that needs to be sent. With image compression a computer analyzes each frame in the series of images that make up the video signal. A program called an algorithm identifies the parts of the picture that change from frame to frame. Only the parts of the image that change are important,

Left: A videoconference. Using a special telephone, you can see the person you speak to.

and the image-compression program ignores all the parts that have stayed the same. It makes sure that only the changing sections are sent. A decompression program at the receiving end expands the compressed signal back into moving images.

Easy to use

Modern videoconferencing equipment can now be attached to a personal computer using a small video camera. Images are sent to the computer's video capture board, processed, and compressed before being sent.

The Integrated Services Digital Network (ISDN) has helped speed up video transmission and improve image quality. ISDN converts the telephone system from an analog system to a faster, digital system. This means that more information can be sent.

Video telephones feature a small color screen that shows the image of the caller. The screen is a liquid crystal display, and the image of the person you are speaking to is picked up by a small camera fitted in the phone and then transmitted. The sound and images are sent in the same way as normal telephone conversations, but they take up a lot more bandwidth. Video telephones were invented more than 50 years ago, but they are still not very popular.

Videophone technology has been available for a long time. This "visiophone" is from 1939.

Email and the Internet

The Internet is a network of computers around the world that connects businesses, governments, companies, universities, and many other users. Between 1990 and 2000 the Internet was the fastest-growing communication system that humankind had ever known.

The Internet uses the telephone network to connect computers to each other. The Internet is based on the Advanced Research Project Agency Network (ARPANET) that was designed to make a communications network that would still be able to work after a nuclear war. The Internet itself began in 1984 to allow universities in the United States to share their information with each other using five regional computer centers.

Personal computers are linked to the Internet through a modem. It communicates directly with an internet service provider (ISP). The ISP is similar to a normal telephone switchboard, and it provides the link from the computer to the Internet location. ISPs connect to other, larger ISPs to access the location.

World of the web

The World Wide Web (www) is the system used for publishing information on the Internet. World Wide Web files are all coded as a standard language called hypertext mark-up language (HTML). This coded language can store not only words but pictures and moving images.

Every Web page has a uniform resource locator (URL), which is its own unique address. Programs called browsers find these URLs. They break them down into three parts in the same way a telephone exchange recognizes the numbers dialed on a phone. The first section is known as the protocol

This laptop computer has a combined telephone and modem on it—you could use it anywhere.

(e.g., http), and it tells the browser the type of data to be sent. The second part is the server name (e.g., www.insideatelephone.com/). It tells the browser where to look for the URL. The final part of the address relates directly to the particular file (e.g., pictures.html and internet.html).

Electronic mail or email is messages sent electronically from computer to computer via the telephone network. Email is designed so that you can send a message from any computer that will be understood by any other computer. An email message is typed and then sent via a modem to an ISP. That ISP sends it to the recipient's ISP. The person receiving the message uses their modem to dial into their ISP and retrieves the message.

Above: When you are on the Internet, you can even use your computer as a special telephone.

Below: A modem. It connects your computer to a telephone line.

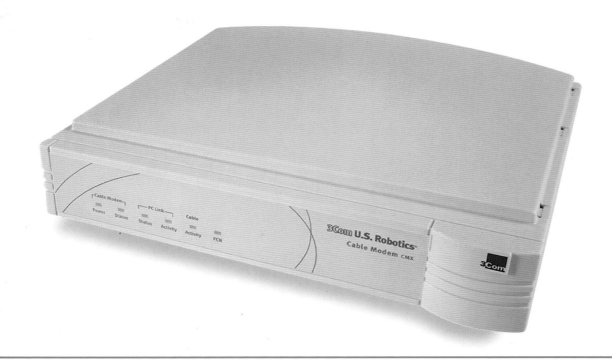

The future of telecommunications

The popularity of the Internet has meant that telephone companies have come under pressure to improve their networks. People want more information, more speed, and better quality.

The development of the mobile telephone means that callers are no longer restricted to using telephones just in buildings. Cellular phones are connected to a communication system by radio waves. The areas covered by the phones are divided into "cells" about 2 miles (3km) across, which each have a low-power transmitter. The mobile telephone network is also expanding because of new low-orbit satellites.

They are nearer Earth than other communications satellites and direct calls through other satellites to a receiver.

Fiber-optic cables are replacing copper wires as the main way of sending telephone communications. A new project known as Project Oxygen is intended to lay 200,000 miles (320,000 km) of fiber-optic cable linking 171 countries. It will be able to carry 30 times as much information as a copper cable. These fiber-optic cables can carry many more signals at the same time, and this means that more information can be sent. At present most fiber-optic cables carry 8 signals, but it is expected that 100 signals can be transmitted through one fiber-optic link.

Audio (sound) files are regularly sent via the Internet. New technology means that using a PC and the Internet could replace the telephone as the main system of communication.

This machine can be used to speak to people, surf the Internet, and send email.

You can write on the screen of this phone—it learns to understand your handwriting—and you can send messages via email when you have written them.

Internet telephony allows people to speak through microphones on their computers and hear the reply through the speakers.

Break the language barrier

Real-time language translation is currently being developed for telephones. It is a system for phone calls in which the caller speaks a different language from the person that they called. When the people speak to each other on the telephone, a computer translates both languages at the same time. The translation is then relayed using a synthesized voice, which keeps the tone of voice of the caller.

Television pictures are being sent digitally through fiber-optic cables. This means that your computer could become the center for all of your communication needs. The huge amount of information that can be sent through the telephone system means that people who work may not even need to visit their offices any more as the home office becomes the center of all their communication. They will be able to save many hours' travel time each day.

This telephone uses satellites to communicate with people around the world.

Glossary

ALGORITHM—a computer program that identifies the changes in a video picture.

ANALOG—signal sent as electrical code rather than digital code.

ANALOG-TO-DIGITAL CONVERTOR—device for changing electrical signals into digital code.

BANDWIDTH—the amount of information that can be sent over a telephone line is measured in bandwidth. The higher it is, the better.

BIT—one single-digit binary code number, eight of which make up a byte.

BYTE—one 8-digit binary code number.

CHARGE-COUPLED DEVICE (CCD)—electronic device for reproducing images electronically. Commonly found in fax machines, video cameras, and videophones.

CONDUCTOR—a device that conducts electricity.

DIGITAL—a measurement made up of single on or off values.

DIGITAL COMMUNICATIONS PROTOCOLS—instructions used in a digital communications network.

DUAL-TONE MULTIFREQUENCY SIGNALING—system of sound pulses used in touch tone dialing.

ELECTROMECHNICAL SWITCHGEAR—machinery used in older telephone exchanges to connect a caller to a number that they dialed.

FIBER-OPTIC CABLE—a cable made from thin strands of glass that carry digital code as light.

FOIL-ELECTRET MICROPHONE—a telephone microphone that uses electrically charged foil to convert sound to electricity.

FREQUENCY-DIVISION MULTIPLEXING—system for combining a number of telephone calls sent as analog signals.

IMAGE COMPRESSION—reducing the amount of image in videoconferencing to reduce the amount of signal needed.

INTEGRATED SERVICES DIGITAL NETWORK (ISDN)—internationally agreed system for sending digital signals along optical fibers.

INTERNET SERVICE PROVIDER (ISP)—internet "switchboard" that provides the link from a computer to Internet locations.

LOCAL LOOP—a network of telephones in one area all connected to a switch at a central office.

MICROWAVES—high-frequency radio waves used to transmit telephone signals.

MODEM (MODULATOR/DEMODULATOR)—a device for connecting computers to telephone lines. The modem changes a computer's signal, by slowing it down, so that it can travel over telephone lines.

MULTIPLEXING—combining telephone signals as they are sent.

PIXEL—a very small dot, many of which together make up a picture.

PULSE-CODE MODULATION (PCM)—the flow of current according to a digital code.

SCANNER—device on a fax for breaking down documents into pixels.

SUBSCRIBER LOOP CARRIER (SLC)—small box or vault that converts the initial signals from a telephone into digital code.

T OR T1 CARRIER—cable that combines 24 twisted pairs of wires from telephones. It can carry a lot of telephone calls.

TIME-DIVISION MULTIPLEXING—system for combining a number of telephone calls sent as digital signals.

TRUNK—the linking cable between two local telephone loops.

FURTHER INFORMATION

Books to read:
The Story of Alexander Graham Bell by Margaret Davidson and Stephen Marchesi; Gareth Stevens, Milwaukee, WI, 1997.

Turning Point Inventions: The Telephone by Sarah Gearhart and Toby Welles; Atheneum, New York, NY, 1999.

Web sites to look at:
http://www.att.com/technology/forfun/
http://www.cavejunction.com/phones/
http://www.telephonepioneers.com/

Museum to visit:
Georgia Rural Telephone Telephone Museum Leslie, GA.
http://sowega.net/~museum/

Telephones have changed a lot since the 1940s, when this phone was built.

Index

PICTURE CREDITS Brother UK 20t **BT Telecommunications** 18tl 24t **3Com Corporation** 27b **Corbis** 4bl Bettmann, 4tr Bettmann, 5tr Bettmann, 9tl Todd Gipstein, 10t Philip Gould, 12r Lawrence Manning, 21tr Bettmann; 29t and cover Reuters Newmedia Inc. **Sylvia Cordaiy Photo Library** 13bl Geoffrey Taunton, 14t Les Gibbon **Ericsson** 26r, 28bl, 29br **Global Marine Systems** 15tl **Hulton Getty** 3t, 18bl, 19tr, 25b, 30b **Image Bank** 22t Andrea Pistolesi **Kyocera Corporation** 3b, 24bl **Museum of Science and Technology, Milan** 21br **Net2Phone** 27tr **Peter Newark's American Pictures** 9br; 11tl **Science Photo Library** 15br, 16tr and cover Geoff Tompkinson Siemens, 13t and cover Joseph Singer, 17br **TELeasy Corporation** 23b (t-top b-bottom r-right l-left c-center)